VARANA TRAVEL GUIDE 2024

**Ancient Charms and Modern
Marvels: Varanasi's Allure**

Philip Mablood

TABLE OF CONTENTS

Introduction

Welcome to Varanasi

Welcome to Varanasi: A Timeless Tapestry of Tradition and Spirituality

Located in the northern Indian state of Uttar Pradesh, Varanasi is a city steeped in spiritual allure and ancient charm. It is nestled along the banks of the sacred Ganges River. Varanasi, sometimes referred to as Kashi or Banaras, is one of the world's oldest cities still in continuous occupation, with a 5,000-year history.

History and Heritage

The history of Varanasi is a tapestry made of historical accounts, myths, and legends. According to legend, this ancient city was founded by the Hindu deity Lord Shiva. Varanasi has been a center of learning, culture, and spirituality for more than 3,000 years, so its age is frequently compared to eternity itself.

The city has seen the birth and spread of profound spiritual teachings, the rise and fall of empires, and the convergence of various cultures. The paths trace the footsteps of the ancient scholars, sages, poets, and philosophers who came here for enlightenment.

Spiritual Significance

In Varanasi, spirituality is ingrained in all facets of daily life. This mysterious city's heart and soul are the ghats, the set of steps that descend to the Ganges. In search of spiritual comfort and rejuvenation, pilgrims and seekers gather here every day to participate in purification rites, prayers, and sacred ceremonies. Observing the captivating Ganga Aarti, a ceremonial sacrifice to the river, inspires wonder and respect.

The Ghats and the Ganges: A Sacred Union

The Varanasi Ghats are a gathering place for a wide range of experiences and feelings. With the Ganges relaxing in the background, the ghats come alive as the sun rises, with devotees carrying out their morning rituals and yoga enthusiasts reciting asanas. The ghats come alive at dusk with the enchanting Ganga Aarti, a must-see event that represents the divine bond between humanity and the holy river. The event features flickering lamps, chants, and rhythmic movements.

The Ganges, which is frequently praised as Varanasi's lifeline, is more than just a physical river; it represents eternal flow and spiritual purity. Immersion in the waters of the sacred site is considered by pilgrims as a means of achieving spiritual emancipation from the cycle of rebirth and forgiveness of sins. This is known as moksha.

Cultural Melting Pot

Varanasi is a thriving kaleidoscope of cultures, customs, and artistic expressions rather than just a center for spirituality. Its ancient temples, each telling a story of devotion and architectural wonder, line its winding, winding streets. The city's bazaars are a veritable gold mine of fine handicrafts, elaborate jewelry, and handwoven silks that showcase the craftsmanship that has been passed down through the generations.

Culinary Delights and Traditional Arts

Varanasi's culinary repertoire tantalizes the sense of taste. The city offers a gastronomic journey as rich as its history, from the delicious street food served in the busy alleys to the lavish vegetarian feasts in its local eateries.

The city preserves and spreads its cultural legacy by embracing a variety of art forms, including dance, classical music, and handloom textiles. Its yearly cultural festivals, which honor the artistic heritage that flourishes amid spiritual fervor, draw artists and enthusiasts from all over the world.

Varanasi Today

Varanasi is a city that embraces modernity without losing sight of its historical roots. The city's dynamic personality is reflected in the contrast between its historic temples and its bustling tech districts. Ancient buildings and modern infrastructure live in harmony together, resulting in a special fusion of traditional charm and modern energy.

Get ready to be mesmerized by a city that is more than just a place to visit; as you travel through the serene ghats, busy marketplaces, and hallowed lanes of Varanasi, you will truly be experiencing something extraordinary. With its mystique, spirituality, and cultural diversity, Varanasi invites you to become a part of its timeless story a story that exists outside of time and space and promises to leave an enduring impression on your soul.

Here in Varanasi, history, spirituality, and the timeless charm of a city that has withstood the test of time are revealed around every corner.

What Makes Varanasi Special

Millions of people have a special place in their hearts and minds for Varanasi, which is frequently referred to as the spiritual capital of India. Varanasi is a unique place to visit for several reasons:

Spiritual Epicenter

For Hindus everywhere, Varanasi represents spirituality and religious significance. Numerous temples, ashrams, and shrines can be found throughout the city, and each one has spiritual and historical significance. The Ganges River, revered as a sacred and cleansing body of water, enhances Varanasi's spiritual atmosphere.

Cultural Tapestry

The city is a mingling pot of many artistic expressions, customs, and cultures. With centuries-old traditions of handloom textiles, classical music, dance, and crafts, Varanasi has a rich cultural legacy. A glimpse of the traditional arts and crafts that survive despite modern influences can be found in its bustling bazaars.

Ghats and the Ganges

One thing that makes Varanasi special is the ghats that line the banks of the Ganges River. These steps function as preludes to regular rituals, spiritual exercises, and group activities. Awe and reverence are evoked when one witnesses the sunrise or sunset rituals along the ghats, particularly the captivating Ganga Aarti.

Historical Significance

The history of Varanasi is rich and extends over thousands of years. Throughout history, it has drawn scholars, philosophers, and seekers as a hub for education, philosophy, and cross-cultural exchange. The city's charm is enhanced by the old buildings and alleyways that tell stories of its glorious past.

Life and Death

Varanasi is known for its unique perspective on the life-death cycle. Hindus hold that moksha, or freedom from the cycle of life and death is granted by dying in Varanasi and being cremated on the banks of the Ganges. For those looking for spiritual salvation, the city is therefore a must-visit location.

Timeless Traditions

The city has a distinct fusion of tradition and modernity thanks to the centuries-old customs and rituals that have been maintained. The lively marketplaces, ancient rituals, and customs of Varanasi provide an insight into the enduring customs that have stood the test of time.

Spiritual Quest

Varanasi is a haven for people pursuing self-discovery and spiritual enlightenment. An environment that is favorable to reflection and development is created by the city's spiritual energy, the presence of knowledgeable gurus, and the devotional atmosphere.

Symbol of Continuity

Varanasi continues to stand for perseverance and continuity in the face of changing times. It has seen empires come and go, but its fundamental nature has not changed. The city creates a harmonious fusion of the old and the new by embracing modernity while maintaining its historical roots.

Essentially, the unique experiences Varanasi provides to each visitor seeking a deeper connection with tradition, spirituality, and the essence of India are what make the city so alluring. These experiences are seamlessly integrated with spirituality, culture, and history.

How to Use This Guide

Here's a summary of how to make the most of the contents of this guide to Varanasi so that you can explore it more fully:

1. Sections Overview

This guide's sections each provide particular insights into various facets of Varanasi.

2. Navigation

Introduction: Learn everything there is to know about the essence, importance, and unique qualities of Varanasi.

Exploration: Investigate the spiritual facets, historical significance, cultural mosaic, and distinctive experiences of the city.

Practical Information: Learn about lodging, transit, safety advice, manners, and must-know words.

Conclusion: Summarize your experience with closing observations and insights.

3. Customize Your Exploration

Spiritual Exploration: Visit the temples, ghats, and rituals to delve into Varanasi's spiritual core.

Cultural Immersion: Take in the vibrant local culture by going to markets, and art galleries, and experiencing customs that are unique to the area.

Practical Planning: To ensure a relaxing and secure stay, make use of the practical information provided.

4. Comprehensive Details

Historical Insights: Discover the evolution of Varanasi, its rich past, and the importance of its heritage sites.

Cultural Delights: Explore the culinary delights, traditional arts, music, and dance forms of the city.

Activities and Experiences: To make the most of your trip, find suggestions for particular events, day trips, and activities.

5. Local Interaction

Engage with Locals: Talk to people in the area to learn about their customs and way of life as well as to obtain insider knowledge for a genuine experience.

Respect Cultural Norms: To guarantee a courteous and enlightening visit, familiarize yourself with the customs and etiquette of the area.

6. Create Your Itinerary

Plan Your Days: Make a schedule by choosing experiences, places to see, and things to do based on your interests and free time.

Blend Experiences: For a comprehensive Varanasi experience, combine cultural indulgence with spiritual exploration.

7. Reflection and Implementation

Apply Insights: Apply the insights and knowledge you've learned from the guide as you explore.

Reflect on Experiences: Spend some time thinking back on the profound insights and experiences you gained from your trip to Varanasi.

You can ensure that your visit to Varanasi is a combination of spirituality, culture, and historical enrichment by making good use of this guide to help you create a memorable and immersive experience.

Getting to Know Varanasi

History of Varanasi

With a rich and distinguished past spanning millennia, Varanasi is a city that embodies time itself. Varanasi is a cradle of civilization and spirituality, with a history entwined with ancient India and origins shrouded in myth and legend. The purpose of this story is to examine Varanasi's historical tapestry and chart its development from antiquity to the present.

Mythical Origins and Early History

According to legend, Varanasi is one of the world's oldest continuously inhabited cities, having been founded by Lord Shiva, one of the main deities in Hinduism. The Varuna and the Assi rivers meet at this location, giving rise to the city's name, which is also known as

Kashi, which translates to "City of Light," or Banaras.

Varanasi's early history is rich in references to ancient Hindu epics and scriptures, such as the Rigveda, which is among the world's oldest books. During the Vedic era, it was an important hub for learning and spiritual enlightenment that promoted the interchange of ideas in philosophy, religion, and knowledge.

Flourishing as a Center of Learning and Spirituality

The importance of Varanasi grew under the rule of several different dynasties, such as the Mauryas, Guptas, and Mughals. The city flourished as a center of education, culture, and spirituality under these rulers. In the temples and ashrams of Varanasi, sages, philosophers, and scholars gathered to engage in discussions, debates, and the quest for knowledge.

Varanasi saw tremendous breakthroughs in astronomy, mathematics, literature, art, and other disciplines during the Gupta Empire's heyday. The city developed into a hub for creative and intellectual pursuits, greatly enhancing India's cultural legacy.

Invaders and Empires: Varanasi Through Dynastic Shifts

Throughout history, the city has experienced multiple invasions and changes in leadership. It saw empires come and go, each leaving their imprint on the cultural fabric of the city. Numerous monuments and buildings that still stand as reminders of the Muslim dynasty's rule in Varanasi are the result of their patronage of the city's arts and architecture, especially that of the Mughals.

Cultural Synthesis and Architectural Marvels

Varanasi's magnificent architecture is a synthesis of different eras and influences. The city is home to a large number of temples, ghats, and structures with a wide variety of architectural styles, from the Mughal era and later dynasties to the ancient Gupta period. Even though it has undergone multiple reconstructions over the centuries, the Kashi Vishwanath Temple, which is dedicated to Lord Shiva, is still regarded as a significant religious site and architectural marvel.

Spiritual Significance and Ritualistic Practices

Varanasi has a spiritual significance that is beyond space and time. It is thought that one can achieve freedom from the cycle of reincarnation by passing away in Varanasi and being cremated on the Ganges ghats. The ghats are the center of many ceremonies, rituals, and spiritual practices. The city's intense spirituality is demonstrated by the daily Ganga Aarti, a captivating ceremony led by priests beside the banks of the river.

Varanasi: Modernity Amidst Tradition

Varanasi embraced modern advancements while preserving its

cultural legacy as the world entered the modern era. As a hub for tourism, education, and spirituality, the city is still thriving. The city's historic charm and customs are preserved despite the addition of contemporary infrastructure, resulting in a distinctive fusion of the two.

The history of Varanasi is a tapestry woven with strands of spirituality, culture, wisdom, and fortitude. It serves as a tangible example of India's rich spiritual and cultural heritage. Varanasi continues to be a timeless city that enthralls tourists with its historical treasures and invites them to discover the spirit of ancient India, despite its mythical beginnings and contemporary vibrancy.

Geographical Overview

Situated on the banks of the holy Ganges River, Varanasi is located in the northern Indian state of Uttar Pradesh.

Its location, with the Ganges River encircling it on the western side, greatly adds to its cultural, religious, and historical significance.

Location and Topography

Varanasi is located in the northernmost region of the state and covers an area of about 82 square kilometers (32 square miles). It is roughly 800 kilometers (500 miles) southeast of New Delhi, the capital of India, and about 320 kilometers (200 miles) southeast of Lucknow, the state capital.

The Ganges River meanders majestically along the western edge of the comparatively flat city. There are many ghats (a flight of steps that descend to the riverbank) dotting Varanasi's landscape, each with its own special cultural, religious, or historical significance.

River Ganges: Lifeline of Varanasi

The Ganges is the central feature of Varanasi's geography and spiritual life; it is frequently worshiped as a goddess and is sacred in Hinduism. It is more than just a physical river; it is essential to the daily life and identity of the city. The river draws both pilgrims and tourists as a location for a variety of religious rites, ceremonies, and events.

Climate: The humid subtropical climate of Varanasi is marked by hot summers, moderate winters, and a monsoon season. March through June are the hottest months of the year, with highs of over 40 degrees Celsius (104 degrees Fahrenheit). From July to September, there is intense rainfall and high humidity during the monsoon season.

The more agreeable months of November through February are known as the winters when temperatures typically range from 5 to 15 degrees Celsius (41 to 59 degrees Fahrenheit). Because it offers a break from the scorching summer heat, this time of year is good for tourism.

Connectivity and Access

There are numerous ways to get from Varanasi to other locations. Major cities in India and overseas can reach the Lal Bahadur Shastri International Airport, which accommodates both domestic and international flights. One of the busiest train stations in the area is Varanasi Junction, which is part of the city's well-connected rail system.

Taxis, buses, cycle rickshaws, and auto rickshaws are the main modes of local transportation in the city that make it easier to get between different attractions, markets, and places of worship.

Varanasi's identity and cultural fabric are shaped by its location on the banks of the Ganges River. The city's level terrain, entwined with the holy river, offers a distinctive setting for cultural events, historical exploration, and religious rites. Travelers are guaranteed accessibility thanks to its connectivity, which enables them to fully immerse themselves in Varanasi's rich history and geography.

Climate and Best Times to Visit

There are three distinct seasons in Varanasi's humid subtropical climate: summer, monsoon, and winter. The ideal times to visit the city to guarantee a comfortable and pleasurable stay are greatly influenced by the weather.

Summer (March to June)
Climate:
Varanasi experiences intensely hot and muggy summers, with highs frequently reaching over 40 degrees Celsius (104 degrees Fahrenheit).

Conditions: Many travelers may find outdoor exploration uncomfortable during these months due to the intense heat.

Activities: Religious celebrations like Holi and Ram Navami take place during this time, providing interesting cultural experiences despite the heat.

Monsoon (July to September)

Climate: Varanasi experiences high humidity and significant rainfall during the monsoon season.

Conditions: Although the rain relieves the summer heat, heavy downpours can impede sightseeing and outdoor activities.

Ganges River: During this period, the river swells, enhancing its scenic beauty but also creating unpredictability in boat rides and riverbank activities.

Winter (October to February)

Climate: Varanasi experiences its most comfortable winters, with highs of 5 to 15 degrees Celsius (41 to 59 degrees Fahrenheit).

Conditions: It's perfect for comfortably exploring the city's markets, ghats, and attractions thanks to the cool, dry weather.

Festivals: The lively atmosphere is further enhanced by the numerous cultural celebrations that take place during the winter, such as Diwali and Dev Deepawali.

Best Time to Visit Varanasi

Winter, from October to February, is usually the best time to visit Varanasi. This time of year has nice weather, which is ideal for seeing the city's sites, participating in cultural events, and taking boat rides on the Ganges without worrying about being too hot or too wet.

It can also be advantageous to travel in the shoulder seasons, which are late autumn (November) or early spring (February to March), though the weather may be a little bit colder or warmer than it is during the peak winter months.

The winter months, especially from October to February, offer the best weather for visitors looking for a relaxing and pleasurable trip to Varanasi. During these months, visitors can fully enjoy the spiritual, cultural, and historical offerings of the city without worrying about being affected by intense heat or heavy precipitation.

Cultural Significance

Varanasi's cultural significance is timeless, weaving together traditional, artistic, and spiritual elements to create a tapestry. The following are the main factors that add to Varanasi's enormous cultural significance:

Spiritual Epicenter

As the holiest city in Hinduism, Varanasi has great spiritual significance. It is thought that a trip to Varanasi and a dip in the Ganges' holy waters can purify the soul and bring about spiritual salvation. Temples, ghats, and ashrams abound throughout the city; they are all sites of religious significance and draw pilgrims from all over the world.

The Ghats: Centers of Spiritual Activity

The hub of Varanasi's spiritual activities is the ghats along the Ganges River.

These steps serve as a foundation for numerous ceremonies, rituals, and daily prayers. Ablutions, meditation, and religious activities are performed by pilgrims, who add to the lively spiritual atmosphere of the city.

Rituals and Ceremonies

Varanasi is well known for its intricate ceremonies and rituals held beside the rivers. The captivating daily Ganga Aarti ceremony, which involves lamps, chants, and prayers offered to the Ganges, embodies the spirit of spirituality and devotion. The city's connection to the cycle of life and death is reflected in other rituals, such as the funeral rites performed at the cremation ghats.

Cultural Heritage and Arts

The city has a thriving classical music and dance scene, as well as handloom fabrics, crafts, literature, and other cultural traditions. With poets, weavers, musicians, and artists all adding to Varanasi's artistic heritage, the city has served as a breeding ground for a variety of artistic expressions. The exquisitely woven Banarasi silk sarees, made with threads of gold and silver, are known throughout the world for their artistry.

Festivals and Celebrations

Varanasi's cultural landscape is enriched with color and vibrancy as a result of the many festivals celebrated there throughout the year. Festivities such as Diwali, Holi, Dev Deepawali, and others are observed with immense enthusiasm and magnificence. Both residents and visitors can fully immerse themselves in the city's festive spirit and cultural heritage during these celebrations.

Timeless Traditions

The ancient practices and traditions of the city have been handed down through the ages and preserved for centuries. Varanasi's rich cultural traditions are what keeps the city alive, from the daily rituals at the ghats to the ceremonies held in temples and the busy marketplaces full of handcrafted goods.

Because of its history as the birthplace of spirituality, creativity, and ageless customs, Varanasi has great cultural significance. It acts as a melting pot where culture and spirituality converge to create an ambiance that piques the senses and entices guests to experience its rich cultural legacy. The city's ingrained traditions, ceremonies, and creative expressions all contribute to its status as an important Indian cultural hub.

Exploring Varanasi's Spiritual Essence

The Ghats of Varanasi

The ghats of Varanasi are an essential component of the city's social, cultural, and spiritual fabric, serving as a metaphor for its heart and soul. The riverfront steps that line the banks of the holy Ganges River are extremely important and have many uses, which adds to Varanasi's special allure.

Spiritual Significance

There are about eighty ghats in Varanasi, each with a unique identity and religious significance. Numerous religious ceremonies, rituals, and spiritual pursuits take place on these ghats. Here, pilgrims and followers congregate to conduct ablutions, make prayers, and submerge themselves in the Ganges' sacred waters to achieve spiritual purification.

Ceremonial Practices

The Ganga Aarti, a magnificent performance that takes place every day at dusk, is one of the main rituals that take place at the ghats. Priests use lamps, incense, and rhythmic chanting to offer prayers to the river during this enthralling ritual. During this ceremony, thousands of lamps are thrown into the river and afloat, creating a stunning sight that represents the deep respect for the Ganges.

Varied Activities

Every ghat has a unique personality and meaning. Certain ghats, like the Manikarnika and Harishchandra ghats, are used for cremation ceremonies and are associated with particular rituals. Yoga is practiced at other ghats and meditation, while others organize festivals, religious processions, and cultural events.

Historical and Cultural Heritage

Many ghats, some of which date back centuries, have a rich historical past.

These ghats' architecture is a blend of different eras and styles, from more modern buildings to older styles. These steps are lined with buildings that are historically significant and exhibit exquisite craftsmanship, such as temples, palaces, and pavilions.

Social and Cultural Hubs

The ghats are hubs of social interaction in addition to being significant religious and spiritual locations. The ghats are popular with both locals and tourists for strolls, conversations, rituals, and just taking in the atmosphere. People from all backgrounds congregate in the ghats, which act as gathering spots and promote a sense of community.

Economic Activities

In addition to their cultural and spiritual significance, the ghats promote economic activity. Tourists frequently take boat rides along the riverbanks, which provide expansive views of the cityscape and the ghats. The ghats are also thriving commercial hubs, with merchants offering street food, souvenirs, and religious goods.

Varanasi's ghats are more than just a set of steps that lead to the river; they are a symbol of the city's culture, spirituality, and communal life. Witnessing the convergence of spirituality and everyday life along the holy Ganges River, Varanasi has long attracted pilgrims, tourists, and seekers from all over the world. These riverfront embankments are testaments to this.

The Ganges: Sacred River of Life

In Indian culture, spirituality, and daily life, the Ganges River, also known as the "Ganga Mata" or simply "Ganga," is highly revered. It is much more than just a physical body of water; to millions of people, it represents spiritual purity, nourishment, and a vital link to their culture.

Spiritual Reverence

In Hinduism, the Ganges is revered as a goddess and worshiped as a source of purity and life. Its waters are thought to possess supernatural abilities that can atone for transgressions and grant spiritual freedom. It is believed that bathing in the Ganges is a purifying act, and a large number of pilgrims come to Varanasi just to dip into its sacred waters.

Cultural and Historical Significance

India's historical and cultural landscape has been significantly shaped by the river. Its banks have seen the growth of many ancient cities, including Varanasi, as well as important historical occurrences and the rise and fall of civilizations. Many old books and scriptures praise the Ganges for its holiness and virtues, saying that its waters have mythical beginnings.

Rituals and Ceremonies

Thousands of religious ceremonies and rituals are conducted daily on the banks of the Ganges River. At the ghats along its banks, devotees congregate to perform rituals, light lamps, and offer prayers. Reverberating along the riverbanks is the Ganga Aarti, a grand ritual that is performed with lamps and hymns, signifying the enduring bond between humanity and divinity.

Source of Livelihood

In addition to being a sacred river, the Ganges provides millions of people who live along its path with food and water. It acts as a transportation route, supplies water for irrigation, and supports agricultural activities. Its waters are essential to the livelihoods of fishing communities, who support the local economy and way of life.

Environmental Concerns

The Ganges faces environmental issues like pollution, industrial waste, and population pressure despite its spiritual and cultural significance. The river is being preserved and cleaned, with several governmental and non-governmental projects intended to restore its ecological balance and purity.

A representation of India's diverse range of customs and beliefs, the Ganges River is a symbol of spirituality, purity, and cultural legacy. Its significance extends beyond national borders, touching millions of lives and eliciting respect, adoration, and reverence from people everywhere. The Ganges continues to be a vital component of India's cultural identity, representing the eternal essence of life itself and carrying the spiritual hopes and dreams of innumerable people.

Temples and Religious Sites

Varanasi is well known for its numerous temples and other places of worship, all of which contribute to the city's rich cultural diversity and have great spiritual significance. Here are a few of Varanasi's well-known temples and holy sites:

Kashi Vishwanath Temple

Significance: Often referred to as the Golden Temple, Kashi Vishwanath Temple is devoted to Lord Shiva and is considered one of the holiest places in Hinduism.

Architecture: Each year, millions of devotees are drawn to the temple by its elaborate design and gold-plated spire.

Rituals: To invoke spirituality and devotion, the temple performs several rituals, such as Aarti and Rudrabhishek.

Sankat Mochan Hanuman Temple

Devotion: The Sankat Mochan Hanuman Temple is devoted to Lord Hanuman and is thought to have been established by the saint Tulsidas in the sixteenth century.

Spiritual Aura: Well-known for its calm atmosphere and spiritual vitality, it draws followers looking for consolation and blessings.

Durga Temple (Durga Kund Mandir)

Goddess Durga: This 18th-century structure, which honors Goddess Durga, is characterized by a striking red color scheme.

Festivals: During Navratri, the temple holds lavish celebrations that draw worshippers from all over.

Tulsi Manas Temple

Cultural Heritage: Built on the spot where Tulsidas wrote the epic poem Ramcharitmanas, which tells the story of Lord Rama's life.

Artistic Depictions: The walls are adorned with scenes from the epic and verses from the Ramcharitmanas.

Bharat Mata Temple:

Unique Concept: An iconic symbol of India's diversity and unity, the temple is devoted to Mother India.

Innovative: The temple has a marble relief map of India carved on it rather than the usual deities.

New Vishwanath Temple (Birla Temple)

Modern Marvel: An architectural wonder composed of white marble that offers a modern take on Hindu temple design.

Spiritual Space: The temple, which honors Lord Shiva, has elaborate sculptures and carvings.

Other Religious Sites

Tulsi Ghat: Consecrated in honor of the esteemed poet Tulsidas, the site is named for the saint.

Assi Ghat: Known for its calm atmosphere, this location is thought to be where the Ganges and the Assi rivers converge.

The religious buildings and temples of Varanasi showcase a variety of architectural styles and spiritual convictions. In addition to being houses of worship, they are also works of architecture, archives of cultural legacy, and hubs of spiritual energy that beckon tourists and pilgrims to fully experience the spiritual core and cultural diversity of the city.

Rituals and Ceremonies

With its rich spiritual heritage and long history, Varanasi is well known for its many rituals and ceremonies held beside the holy Ganges River. These customs provide an insight into the vibrant culture and intense spirituality that characterize the city. The following are a few well-known ceremonies and rituals:

Ganga Aarti

Spectacular Ritual: Every day at dusk, the intricate and captivating Ganga Aarti ritual is performed.

Synchronized Devotion: Using lamps, incense, and rhythmic chants, priests synchronize their movements along the ghats to conduct the ceremony.

Spiritual Significance: The Ganges is revered and thanked for its divinity and cleansing properties, and the Aarti represents this gratitude.

Subah-e-Banaras (Morning Prayer)

Morning Invocation: The Subah-e-Banaras is a calm morning prayer ritual that is carried out at Assi Ghat.

Chants and Hymns: To start the day with a positive and spiritual attitude, devotees come together to take part in prayers, hymns, and yoga sessions.

Manikarnika Ghat and Harishchandra Ghat

Cremation Ceremonies: These ghats observe the somber and spiritually profound cremation ceremonies.

Beliefs: Hindus hold that cremation at these ghats offers moksha, or salvation, by freeing the soul from the cycle of rebirth.

Pitru Paksha

Ancestral Ritual: An annual ritual known as Pitru Paksha involves devotees making tarpans, or offerings, to their ancestors.

Belief: It is thought that carrying out these rites at this time helps the spirits of the deceased ancestors find peace.

Dev Deepawali

Festival of Lights: Held during the full moon of Kartik month, thousands of lamps are lit along the ghats in observance of this festival.

Grandeur: The lamps that illuminate the ghats reflect the divine connection between humans and gods and create a magical atmosphere.

Akshaya Tritiya Snan

Sacred Bathing: On the auspicious day of Akshaya Tritiya, devotees immerse themselves in the Ganges for a holy dip, which is said to bestow spiritual merit and perpetual prosperity.

The rituals and ceremonies of Varanasi are an essential component of its spiritual and cultural legacy, providing insights into age-old customs and cultivating a profound sense of respect and devotion. These customs, which range from yearly celebrations like Dev Deepawali to daily ceremonies like the Ganga Aarti, capture the spiritual vitality and cultural sanctity of the city and invite guests to experience the timeless essence of Varanasi's spiritual traditions.

Navigating Varanasi's Cityscape

Old City vs. New City

Varanasi, which is sometimes referred to as the spiritual capital of India, exhibits a special duality between its Old City and New City neighborhoods, each of which has its atmospheres, features, and experiences.

Old City (Varanasi)

Ancient Charm: The Old City is a maze of tiny lanes, historic temples, and lively bazaars, all nestled along the banks of the Ganges River.

Spiritual Heart: The city's deep-rooted customs, ceremonies, and spiritual essence are all part of Varanasi's soul.

Historical Significance: Varanasi's rich heritage is reflected in the Old City, which is home to numerous historical landmarks, including revered temples like the Dashashwamedh Ghat and the Kashi Vishwanath Temple.

Cultural Enclave: Offering an immersive cultural experience, the streets are alive with religious ceremonies, lively cultural events, and craftsmen showcasing traditional crafts.

New City (Varanasi)

Modern Facets: Wider roads, well-planned infrastructure, and contemporary amenities give this city, sometimes referred to as the city's urban extension, a more contemporary appearance.

Commercial Hub: It functions as the hub for contemporary businesses, housing complexes, and educational institutions.

Accommodations and Services: In contrast to the Old City's traditional charm, the New City offers a variety of lodging options, dining options, and services to suit a wide range of preferences.

Development and Growth: This area shows how Varanasi has modernized while trying to keep its cultural heritage intact.

Contrasts and Complements

Cultural Dichotomy: The New City represents progress and modernity, while the Old City retains historic rituals, spiritual beliefs, and magnificent architecture.

Harmonious Coexistence: The two regions work well together to allow guests to witness Varanasi's striking but peaceful fusion of history and modernity.

Varied Experiences: While the New City provides comfort, convenience, and a look into modern Varanasi, the Old City offers a spiritual and cultural immersion.

The contrast between Varanasi's Old and New City offers tourists a variety of experiences. The city's spiritual, historical, and cultural legacy is embodied in the Old City, while modernization and development are reflected in the New City. When combined, they create a tapestry that perfectly depicts Varanasi, a city where modern advancement coexists with age-old customs, providing visitors with a rich and varied experience.

Bustling Bazaars and Markets

The vibrant marketplaces and bazaars of Varanasi are sensory overloads of vibrant displays, traditional crafts, fragrant spices, and lively activity. The following are a few of the city's well-known markets and bazaars:

Vishwanath Gali

Specialty: Renowned for religious objects, supplies needed for pujas (worship), and temple offerings.

Attractions: A plethora of shops selling brassware, rudraksha beads, and souvenirs line the market.

Godowlia Market

Diverse Offerings: The Godowlia Market has a diverse selection of goods, such as jewelry, handicrafts, textiles, and saris.

Food Delights: The market's charm is enhanced by food stalls and vendors offering regional specialties like chaat, kachori, and lassi.

Thatheri Bazaar

Metalware Haven: specializes in religious artifacts, decorative items, and brass and copper utensils.

Craftsmanship: Get a glimpse of traditional metalworking by watching artisans create metal objects.

Chowk

Silk Paradise: Known for its exquisitely woven and skillfully crafted Banarasi silk sarees.

Varied Shopping: Provides handcrafted goods, wooden toys, and carpets among other things.

Golghar Market

Textile Hub: A market teeming with textiles, fabrics, and dress materials is the Golghar Market Textile Hub.

Traditional Attire: There are many different outfit options available to visitors, including traditional Indian attire.

The markets and bazaars of Varanasi offer a delightful shopping experience steeped in culture and tradition, catering to a wide range of tastes and preferences. These vibrant markets offer a window into the city's rich legacy and craftsmanship, showcasing everything from handcrafted textiles and delicious street food to religious artifacts and more. Discovering these lively markets is more than just a shopping experience; it's an opportunity to immerse yourself in Varanasi's vibrant energy, rich cultural legacy, and talented artisans' work.

Varanasi's Culinary Delights

The delicious mix of flavors found in Varanasi's cuisine offers a delightful selection of dishes that pay homage to the city's rich history and wide range of influences. Here are a few dishes you simply must try while visiting Varanasi:

Chaat

Kachori Sabzi: Aromatic potato curry served with deep-fried dumplings packed with spiced lentils.

Tamatar Chaat: A tomato-based, tangy, spicy snack topped with chutneys and spices.

Lassi

Malaiyo: A creamy, frothy milk dessert that is typically served in the winter.

Thandai: Popular during festivals like Holi, this refreshing beverage is made with milk, nuts, and spices.

Sweets

Banarasi Paan: A mixture of flavors in a flavored betel leaf preparation that is frequently used as a digestive.

Malai Chop: Rich, creamy treats made with milk, such as malai ki gilori or malai ki launj.

Street Food

Parantha Stalls: Try the renowned aloo (potato) or mixed vegetable stuffed paranthas, which are served with pickles and chutneys.

Samosa: Crispy triangle pastries stuffed with peas, potatoes, and occasionally lentils that have been spiced.

Traditional Cuisine

Baati Chokha: A traditional dish that consists of mashed vegetables (chokha) and baked wheat balls (baati), usually served with ghee.

Bhaang: A unique dish prepared from cannabis leaves that is eaten in certain forms during the Holi festival.

Gourmet Offerings

Thali: Savor a typical Indian dinner of a variety of dishes arranged on a platter to display a range of tastes and textures.

Local Cuisine at Eateries: Sample some of the region's specialties at neighborhood eateries that serve real Varanasi food.

With a delicious blend of flavors, spices, and textures, Varanasi's culinary offerings are a treat for food enthusiasts. Every meal is an unforgettable experience thanks to the city's diverse culinary offerings, which highlight the region's rich cultural legacy and culinary artistry. You can indulge in street food treats, enjoy traditional sweets, or savor local specialties.

Traditional Arts and Crafts

Varanasi is well known for its extensive history of arts and crafts, which features exquisite workmanship that has been handed down through the ages. The city's craftspeople produce beautiful handicrafts, textiles, and artwork. Here are a few examples of Varanasi's traditional crafts and arts:

Banarasi Silk Sarees

Exquisite Weaving: Distinguished by their fine silk fabric, elaborate designs, and gold and silver brocade work.

Heritage Craft: Due to their classic elegance, banarasi sarees are highly sought after for weddings and other special occasions.

Zari and Brocade Work

Metallic Embroidery: Expert weavers use metallic threads to create elaborate designs that elevate fabrics and clothing.

Usage: Zari and brocade work adorns fabrics, shawls, and home decor items, in addition to sarees.

Metalware and Brassware

Traditional Craftsmanship: Beautiful brass cookware, statues, lamps, and religious objects are crafted by artisans.

Intricate Designs: These pieces frequently have intricate carvings and conventional themes.

Wooden Toys and Crafts

Artistic Creations: Talented artisans create lacquer-coated goods, wooden toys, and decorative accents.

Playful and Colorful: The toys frequently feature dolls, animals, and mythological figures.

Carpet Weaving

Fine Craftsmanship: Silk and wool carpets are expertly woven by artisans in Varanasi.

Handwoven Elegance: Carpets come in a range of colors, geometric patterns, and traditional designs.

Musical Instruments

Instrument Crafting: Traditional Indian musical instruments such as the tabla, sitar, and tanpura are crafted by artisans by hand.

Precision and Quality: Varanasi is renowned for creating instruments of the highest caliber and remarkable tone.

Varanasi's handicrafts and arts represent the city's rich cultural legacy with their superb artistry and craftsmanship. The city's artistic soul is reflected in the timeless creations made possible by the continued flourishing of skills passed down through the generations. Discovering the marketplaces and workshops devoted to these crafts provides an insight into Varanasi's elaborate craftsmanship and rich cultural heritage.

Activities and Experiences

Sunrise and Sunset Boat Rides

Boat rides on the Ganges River at dawn and dusk in Varanasi are a captivating and calming experience that offers a distinctive viewpoint of the city's natural beauty and spiritual aura. What to anticipate in these peaceful moments is as follows:

Sunrise Boat Rides

Serene Dawn: As the first light of the day fills the ghats and temples lining the riverbanks, you can watch the city awaken to a new day.

Spiritual Atmosphere: Take in the peaceful, devotional atmosphere created by the locals' spiritual rites and prayers.

Golden Glow: As the sun rises, the river is bathed in a golden glow that captures the enduring allure of Varanasi.

Sunset Boat Rides

Golden Hour: Witness the magnificent spectacle of the sun setting and illuminating the sky in shades of orange, pink, and purple.

Aarti Ceremony: Witness the Ghats come to life with lamps and prayers as you observe the Ganga Aarti ceremony from a boat.

Peaceful Reverence: As the day draws to an end, take in the calm ambiance and see the river change into a tranquil mirror of the city's pious energy.

Highlights of Both Rides

Ghats and Temples: Explore the many ghats and temples that line the river and get a unique perspective of the city's religious and cultural sites.

Local Life: Take in the day-to-day activities along the riverbanks, including pilgrims in deep prayer, priests enacting rituals, and residents taking baths in the sacred waters.

Scenic Beauty: Bask in the breathtaking views of Varanasi's skyline, which perfectly captures the spirit of the historic city set against the Ganges' meandering course.

Recommendations

Timing: Schedule your boat rides for early morning to take in the serene beauty of sunrises or late afternoon to experience the dreamy atmosphere of sunsets.

Boat Options: Select from shared or private boat rides; each provides a unique experience, with private trips enabling more individualized discovery.

Boat rides on the Ganges at sunrise and sunset offer picturesque views and a chance to see the city's spiritual essence emerge in the calm waters of Varanasi. With the help of these rides, guests can connect with Varanasi's timeless charm and spiritual core in a tranquil and immersive experience.

Cultural Performances and Events

Varanasi is a cultural gold mine, with a wide range of exciting shows and activities showcasing the city's rich artistic history and fervent spirituality. The following are a few notable Varanasi cultural events and performances:

Ganga Aarti

Daily Ritual: Held at dusk, the captivating Ganga Aarti is a spiritual ceremony that involves prayers, chants, and lamps at the ghats.

Spectacular Display: The priests coordinate their steps, resulting in a mesmerizing atmosphere by the river.

Classical Music and Dance Performances

Sangeet Sabha: Classical music, including Hindustani classical, Carnatic music, and traditional dance forms, is performed at various sabhas (music societies).

Renowned Artists: Famous dancers and musicians frequently grace audiences in Varanasi with their exquisite performances.

Ram Leela and Natya Utsav

Theatrical Extravaganza: The city comes to life with dramatic enactments depicting folklore and mythological stories during festivals like Natya Utsav and Ram Leela.

Local Participation: The shows are made more authentic and lively by the participation of local actors and enthusiasts.

Devotional Music and Bhajan Recitals

Bhajan Sandhya: Temples and ashrams host spiritual events that include kirtans, devotional music, and bhajan recitals.

Spiritual Atmosphere: Traditional melodies and a calm atmosphere are created by these events.

Festivals and Celebrations

Diwali and Dev Deepawali: The city is illuminated with lamps, fireworks, and cultural events during Diwali and Dev Deepawali, creating a mystical atmosphere.

Holi and Durga Puja: A glimpse into Varanasi's colorful celebrations, these events feature colorful processions, cultural shows, and customary rituals.

Varanasi's cultural events and performances, which combine spirituality, art, and tradition, perfectly capture the essence of the city's rich past. These events allow guests to fully experience Varanasi's alluring atmosphere and vibrant culture while also offering a deeper understanding of the city's cultural tapestry. The timeless appeal of Varanasi's cultural heritage is revealed through these offerings, which range from the majesty of Ganga Aarti to soul-stirring classical music.

Meditation and Yoga Retreats

Renowned for its spiritual vibrancy, Varanasi offers a range of yoga and meditation retreats that offer a calm and peaceful setting for introspection, rest, and spiritual renewal. The following are some choices for yoga and meditation retreats in and near Varanasi:

Sivananda Ashram Yoga and Meditation:

Sivananda Ashram Yoga and Meditation: Offers courses and retreats for those who are seeking enlightenment as well as regular yoga and meditation sessions.

Serene Environment: The ashram offers a serene setting for spiritual activities.

Anand Prakash Ashram

Yoga and Wellness: Provides Hatha yoga, pranayama, meditation, and yogic philosophy as the main topics of their yoga retreats.

Nature Retreat: Located on the outskirts, it offers a tranquil environment for reflection and rest amidst the natural world.

International Yoga and Meditation Centre

Holistic Practices: Offers yoga, meditation, and wellness courses to both novice and seasoned practitioners at the International Yoga and Meditation Center.

Cultural Immersion: Offers the chance to learn about old spiritual traditions and take part in cultural activities.

Osho Meditation Center

Meditation Workshops: Provides workshops and a range of meditation techniques based on Osho's teachings.

Holistic Healing: Emphasizes the use of meditation as a tool for personal development and inner transformation.

Upaya Yoga Center

Yoga and Ayurveda: Offers holistic wellness and spiritual rejuvenation through its yoga and Ayurvedic retreats.

Experienced Instructors: Under the direction of seasoned educators, providing individualized instruction and practice.

Rajghat Besant School Yoga Center

Yoga Courses: Provides short-term yoga courses and retreats in a calm setting.

Cultural Exposure: Situated close to the ghats, Cultural Exposure allows participants to delve into the spiritual and cultural aspects of Varanasi.

Meditation and yoga retreats in Varanasi offer a calm and spiritually enlightening atmosphere for people looking for holistic wellness, self-discovery, and relaxation. These centers provide an opportunity for visitors to immerse themselves in the spiritual ethos of the city and begin a journey of self-transformation, whether it's by exploring meditation practices more deeply, accepting the therapeutic benefits of yoga, or taking part in the serenity of spiritual retreats.

Heritage Walks and Tours

Heritage walks and tours in Varanasi provide an enthralling tour of the city's historic sites, cobblestone alleys, and cultural treasures. The following are some options for Varanasi heritage walks and tours:

Banaras Heritage Walk

Guided Exploration: Guided tours of the old marketplaces, temples, and lanes are provided by experienced guides on organized heritage walks.

Cultural insights: During these immersive walks, learn about the rich history, architecture, and customs of Varanasi.

Varanasi Walking Tours

Customized Tours: Tour operators that provide walking tours that can be customized in Varanasi

Local Experience: designed to delve into particular facets of the city's history. Engage with local communities, explore lesser-known locations, and observe Varanasi's daily life to gain a local perspective.

Ghats Walk

Ghat Exploration: Guided walks around Varanasi's ghats, offering information on the customs, spiritual meanings, and historical anecdotes connected to each one.

Scenic Experience: Experience the scenic beauty of the Ganges River, its temples, and the lively activities that surround it.

Cultural and Historical Tours

Heritage Trails: Excursions that take visitors to famous sites such as the Sarnath Archaeological Site, Durga Temple, and Kashi Vishwanath Temple.

Architectural Marvels: Discover the architectural wonders and rich cultural legacy of Varanasi's palaces, temples, and historic buildings.

Food and Culture Walks

Culinary Exploration: Street food, specialty foods, and culinary traditions of Varanasi are showcased through food-focused walks.

Cultural Immersion: Incorporate learning about the city's customs, rituals, and cultural practices with culinary exploration.

Photography Tours

Photography Expeditions: Guided tours designed for those who love taking pictures; these trips give you the chance to capture the spirit, color, and diversity of the city.

Scenic Vistas: Find charming locations and undiscovered treasures that are perfect for preserving Varanasi's enduring allure.

The immersive experiences offered by Varanasi's heritage walks and tours give visitors a better understanding of the city's rich cultural legacy, architectural wonders, spiritual significance, and customs. Discovering Varanasi's fascinating history and making enduring memories of this vibrant city are encouraged by these tours and walks, which include activities like strolling through its historic lanes, seeing its famous sites, and savoring its delectable cuisine.

Day Trips and Nearby Attractions

Sarnath: Birthplace of Buddhism

Sarnath, a popular pilgrimage site and the birthplace of Buddhism is situated close to Varanasi and is extremely significant. An outline of the historical and cultural significance of Sarnath is provided below:

Historical Importance

First Sermon:

The Dhammacakkappavattana Sutta, also referred to as the "Turning of the Wheel of Dharma," is the name of the first sermon that Lord Buddha gave in Sarnath following his enlightenment in Bodh Gaya.

Deer Park: The Four Noble Truths and the Eightfold Path, which laid the groundwork for Buddhism, were revealed by the Buddha during his sermon there.

Key Attractions

Dhamek Stupa: The Dhamek Stupa is a large, cylindrical structure that marks the location of the Buddha's first sermon. Tourists and pilgrims are drawn to the stupa by its historical significance and elaborate carvings.

Mulagandha Kuti Vihar: A contemporary temple surrounded by peaceful gardens that features exquisite murals portraying the life of the Buddha.

Sarnath Archaeological Museum: Offers insights into Buddhist art and history through its extensive collection of relics, sculptures, and artifacts that were excavated from the site.

Spiritual Significance

Pilgrimage Destination: Sarnath continues to be a significant Buddhist pilgrimage site that draws adherents and academics curious about the history of Buddhism.

Meditative Atmosphere: The calm atmosphere of Sarnath encourages people to think, meditate, and feel the peace that is connected to Buddha's teachings.

Cultural Impact

Spread of Buddhism: The teachings of Buddha were transmitted from Sarnath throughout Asia, and this was largely due to their influence.

Architectural marvels: The monuments and buildings at Sarnath are prime examples of Buddhist and ancient Indian architecture, demonstrating the artistic prowess of the time.

Preservation Efforts

Conservation Initiatives: Constant work to maintain the historical and cultural integrity of the archaeological site and its monuments through preservation and restoration.

UNESCO World Heritage Site: Sarnath, a component of the "Buddhist Monuments at Sanchi," is officially designated as a UNESCO World Heritage Site.

As the starting point of the Buddha's teachings and the dissemination of Buddhism, Sarnath is both a sacred place for Buddhists and an important historical site. It is a must-visit location for anyone looking to delve into the historical and cultural underpinnings of Buddhism and experience its rich spiritual legacy because of its monuments, relics, and spiritual significance.

Ramnagar Fort and Museum

The historic Ramnagar Fort in Varanasi is a well-known attraction that provides a window into the area's royal and cultural past. It is situated on the eastern bank of the Ganges River. An outline of Ramnagar Fort and its museum is provided below:

Historical Significance

Historic Residence: From the 18th century, the fort was the Maharaja of Varanasi's ancestral home.

Architectural Marvel: The fort displays a fusion of influences from various eras thanks to its integration of Mughal and Rajput architectural styles.

Key Features

Museum: The Ramnagar Fort Museum is housed within the fort and features an extensive collection of antiques, weapons, manuscripts, and vintage cars.

Art and Culture: The museum's displays provide information about the artistic, cultural, and historical developments of the area.

Durbar Hall

Royal Court: Inside the fort, the Durbar Hall functioned as the royal audience hall and was decorated with elaborate patterns and antiques.

Cultural Heritage: The region's artifacts showcase its cultural heritage, and visitors can revel in the splendor of the royal court.

Mankameshwar Temple

Sacred Site: The Mankameshwar Temple, devoted to Lord Shiva, is located next to the fort and is visited by both residents and visitors.

Religious Significance: The temple offers a window into Varanasi's religious landscape and lends a spiritual element to the fort's ambiance.

Vintage Boats and Ghats

Boat Collection: The fort displays old boats that are used for celebrations such as Dussehra, giving visitors a taste of local culture.

Scenic Riverfront: The fort's location alongside a river allows visitors to take in the breathtaking views of the Ganges.

Cultural Events

Dussehra Celebrations: Ramnagar Fort serves as the hub for elaborate Dussehra celebrations that include processions, cultural shows, and the Ramlila enactment.

Varanasi's royal past and cultural legacy are preserved in the Ramnagar Fort and its museum. Visitors can learn about the area's royal past, view antique collections, and become fully immersed in Varanasi's cultural fabric by exploring the fort and museum. The fort is an important historical landmark in the city because of its advantageous location by the Ganges, which enhances its charm.

Chunar Fort

Near Varanasi, Chunar Fort is a historic fortification with a colorful past that offers an intriguing fusion of historical significance and architectural beauty. This is a synopsis of Chunar Fort:

Historical Significance

Strategic Stronghold: Historically used as a military stronghold regulating river trade routes, the fort has a strategic location overlooking the Ganges River.

Ancient Roots: The fort has been influenced by several dynasties throughout its history, including the Mauryas, Guptas, Mughals, and British.

Key Features

Architecture: With its imposing walls, gateways, and bastions, the fort demonstrates a fusion of various historical architectural styles.

Ancient Legends: The stone walls of the fort are said to have impressions made by Lord Rama and the fabled Chandrahas sword.

Sonwa Mandap

Notable Structure: One of the fort's main architectural features is the octagonal Sonwa Mandap tower.

Scenic Views: Stunning panoramas of the Ganges and the surroundings are available.

Kali Paltan Mandir

Religious Shrine: The Kali Paltan Mandir, devoted to Goddess Kali, is housed in the fort and is a highly respected location for followers.

Spiritual Atmosphere: The temple's architectural beauty and spiritual atmosphere are both available to visitors.

Chunar Jail

Historical Prison: Known for housing freedom fighters during India's fight for independence, Chunar Jail is located within the fort.

Cultural Significance: The jail's past is linked to India's liberation struggle, which heightens the fort's historical significance.

Cultural Heritage

Local Legends: The fort's cultural significance is derived from its connections to several historical occurrences and legends.

Attraction for Tourists: Attracts history buffs, admirers of architecture, and travelers eager to see historic sites.

Chunar Fort is a monument to Varanasi's rich cultural and historical heritage, combining history, legends, and architectural magnificence. Visitors can have an immersive experience by exploring the fort, which offers architectural wonders, a window into the past of the area, and an understanding of the fort's strategic significance throughout history.

Offbeat Excursions

For daring tourists looking for out-of-the-ordinary adventures, Varanasi provides a plethora of unusual trips that go beyond the typical tourist route. Consider going on the following unusual trips in and around Varanasi:

Rural Village Visits

Countryside Exploration: Explore the countryside by going into the neighboring rural villages to get a sense of the real rural lifestyle and interact with the locals.

Cultural Immersion: Experience a cultural immersion by taking part in customs, interacting with locals, and seeing age-old crafts and customs.

Silk Weaving Workshops

Artisanal Experience: See the elaborate process of creating Banarasi silk sarees by visiting silk weaving workshops located on the outskirts of the city.

Hands-On Experience: Learn how to weave or attempt pattern design from experienced craftspeople.

Aghor Peeth

Spiritual Exploration: Visit Aghor Peeth to learn about Aghori philosophy and practices if you're interested in spiritual or mystical matters.

Insightful Encounters: Through conversations with Aghori Sadhus, learn about Aghori customs, beliefs, and way of life.

Heritage Havelis and Mansions

Architectural Exploration: Discover lesser-known heritage havelis and mansions in Varanasi that offer stunning architecture and historical significance through architectural exploration.

Hidden Gems: Acquire knowledge from local guides about the cultural significance of these little architectural wonders.

River Island Exploration

Journey to River Islands: Discover the Ganges islands, which include Ayodhya and Ramnagar, which have quiet areas and beautiful scenery.

Nature Trails and Picnics: Savor peaceful moments away from the bustle of the city by going on nature walks and picnics.

Sarnath Excursions at Dawn

Early Morning Visit: Visit Sarnath in the early morning to take in the calm atmosphere and spiritual serenity of the place.

Meditative Atmosphere: As the day dawns, spend some time in solitude, practicing meditation, or just taking in the spiritual aura.

The unusual tours available in Varanasi provide a chance to discover little-known aspects of the city's spirituality, culture, and scenic surroundings. These non-traditional travel adventures offer immersive experiences that let visitors explore the region's many offerings in greater detail and make unforgettable memories that go beyond the usual tourist traps.

Practical Information

Accommodation Options

Varanasi offers a variety of lodging choices to suit a wide range of budgets and tastes, from opulent heritage hotels to guesthouses on the cheap. These are a few of the lodging options the city offers.

Heritage Hotels

Palatial Stay: Experience the allure of beautifully renovated palaces or havelis that have been transformed into opulent historical hotels, providing regal lodging with classic design and contemporary conveniences.

Cultural Immersion: Take in the grandeur and history of the city while being treated with the utmost hospitality.

Boutique Hotels

Charming Ambiance: Adorable boutique hotels that combine style, comfort, and individualized attention;

frequently found in historic districts or along the ghats.

Unique Settings: Take a look at smaller estates with unique personalities and cultural influences.

Guesthouses and Homestays

Local Experience: For a more personal and genuine experience, consider staying in a family-run guest house or homestay.

Personalized Hospitality: Be treated with kindness, mingle with residents, and receive insider information about Varanasi.

Budget Hotels and Hostels

Affordable Stays: There are a lot of inexpensive hotels and hostels that provide cozy accommodations at reasonable costs.

Ideal for Backpackers: Ideal for travelers on a tight budget looking for social atmosphere and basic amenities.

Luxury Resorts

Riverside Retreats: Exquisite hotels along the Ganges that provide sumptuous lodging, spa services, and expansive river views.

Tranquil Escapes: Savor calm environs and excellent amenities in an opulent atmosphere.

Ashrams and Spiritual Retreats

Spiritual Experience: A few ashrams provide lodging for guests interested in going on a yoga immersion or spiritual retreat.

Simple Living: For those seeking a peaceful stay, modest lodgings are set in a spiritual environment.

Varanasi offers a wide variety of lodging choices to accommodate different tastes and price ranges. Whatever your preference, the warmth of a homestay, the elegance of heritage hotels, the charm of boutique stays, or the ease of budget lodging, there are lots of options to guarantee a pleasant and unforgettable stay while you explore Varanasi's spiritual and cultural attractions.

Transportation in Varanasi

Varanasi provides a range of transit choices to navigate the city and get to surrounding locations:

Cycle Rickshaws

Local Commute: Commonly utilized for brief trips within cities, particularly in congested areas and small lanes.

Budget-Friendly: An affordable way to visit temples, ghats, and local markets.

Auto Rickshaws

Convenient Commute: This mode of transportation is faster than cycle rickshaws and is available for both short and medium distances.

Negotiate Fare: It's a good idea to talk about the fare in advance as most fares are negotiable.

Taxis

Convenience and Comfort: For longer trips or airport transfers, taxis provide a more secluded and comfortable mode of transportation.

Prepaid Taxis: Fixed fares are guaranteed with prepaid taxi services, which are accessible at the train and airport stations.

E-Rickshaws

Eco-Friendly Ride: E-rickshaws are becoming more and more well-liked as a cost-effective and environmentally friendly way to go short distances.

Electric Vehicles: These vehicles are frequently used for local transportation and help the environment.

Public Buses

City and Inter-City Travel: Varanasi's public bus system connects the city's various neighborhoods and neighboring towns.

Varanasi to Sarnath: For those who wish to visit the Buddhist pilgrimage site, buses run between Varanasi and Sarnath.

Boats

River Transport: Providing beautiful rides and access to different ghats, boats are a traditional mode of transportation along the Ganges River.

Sunrise/Sunset Rides: During sunrise and sunset, you can get a beautiful view of the ghats and rituals.

Rental Services

Bicycle Rentals: If you want to tour the city at your speed, a few stores rent out bicycles.

Car Rentals: You can rent cars with or without drivers to go on customized city tours or excursions to neighboring attractions.

Varanasi offers a wide variety of transit choices to suit various tastes and travel requirements. While discovering the city's cultural and spiritual treasures, visitors can select the form of transportation that best fits their schedule and level of comfort, from the famous boat rides along the Ganges to the practicality of taxis and auto-rickshaws for local commuting.

Safety Tips and Advice

The following safety guidelines and recommendations are for visitors to Varanasi:

Cultural Sensitivity

Respect Local Customs: Varanasi is a vibrant, culturally diverse city. Observe local customs, religious beliefs, and feelings when you visit temples and take part in rituals.

Health and Hygiene

Stay Hydrated: Keep bottled water on hand and drink plenty of it, especially in hot weather.

Food Precautions: Take care when consuming street food; to prevent foodborne illnesses, choose freshly prepared meals and reliable restaurants.

Personal Safety

Valuables and Documents: Safeguard your passports, valuables, and important papers. When touring the city, make use of hidden pouches or hotel safes.

Avoid Isolated Areas: Especially after dark, steer clear of isolated or poorly lit areas.

Transportation Safety

Verified Transportation: Choose licensed auto rickshaws or taxis and make sure the fare is agreed upon before you get in.

Watch Your Belongings: To prevent theft, keep a watch on your property when taking public transportation.

Dress Code and Attire

Appropriate Clothing: Show consideration for the customs of the community by dressing modestly, particularly when visiting places of worship and taking part in rituals.

Health Precautions

Medical Kit: Always keep a simple medical kit on you that includes band-aids, antiseptics, and any prescription drugs you might need.

Mosquito Protection: Use nets or insect repellents to protect yourself from mosquitoes, especially at night and in the evening.

Communication and Navigation

Local SIM Card: To facilitate communication and internet access while visiting, think about getting a local SIM card.

Offline Maps: To navigate the city, either download offline maps or bring a physical map with you.

Emergency Contacts

Emergency Numbers: Keep the phone numbers for local law enforcement, hospitals, and the embassy or consulate of your country close at hand in case of emergency.

Even though Varanasi is a bustling, culturally diverse city, you can still improve your safety and guarantee a hassle-free, pleasurable trip by being aware of your surroundings and taking some precautions. If you take precautions and embrace the city's charm, you should have no trouble fully immersing yourself in its cultural mosaic.

Etiquette and Cultural Norms

When visiting Varanasi, it is imperative to comprehend and honor cultural norms and local etiquette. The following cultural customs should be remembered:

Religious Sites and Practices

Covering Body: When visiting temples and other places of worship, wear modest clothing. When entering temples, take off your shoes and avoid wearing anything too skimpy.

Respectful Behavior: During rituals, keep quiet, abstain from taking pictures when it's forbidden, and heed any instructions from priests or locals.

Greetings and Interactions

Respectful Greetings: Give people a respectful "Namaste" by putting your hands together. Be courteous and speak politely with others.

Asking Permission: Before taking someone's picture, especially one of a local or during a religious ceremony, make sure you have their consent.

Eating Etiquette

Handwashing: Always wash your hands before and after consuming food, particularly in neighborhood restaurants.

Culinary Traditions: Use only your right hand (which is thought to be more hygienic) when eating with your hands; do not use your left hand.

Social Norms

Public Behavior: Refrain from making public shows of affection as they may be interpreted as impolite in conventional settings.

Refrain from Aggression: Keep your cool under pressure and refrain from arguing aloud or acting aggressively in public.

Tipping and Gifts

Tipping Custom: Tipping is not required, but it is appreciated in some situations, such as when tour guides or restaurants provide excellent service.

Gift Giving: When giving gifts, show respect by using both hands to deliver them.

Photography

Respect Privacy: Before snapping pictures of people, especially in remote locations or during religious ceremonies, get their consent.

No Photography Zones: Be mindful of locations, such as some temples or religious ceremonies, where taking pictures is forbidden.

Varanasi culture places a strong emphasis on decency, modesty, and civility. Visitors may maximize their experience and demonstrate respect for the city's rich cultural legacy by dressing appropriately, acting politely, and being aware of local customs. Maintaining these manners guarantees a more seamless and pleasurable engagement with the local populace and their customs.

Essential Phrases and Words

The following are some keywords and phrases in Hindi that visitors to Varanasi may find helpful:

Basic Greetings

Namaste: Greetings or Hello (expressed while putting your hands together)

Aap kaise hain: How are you doing?

Dhanyavaad / Shukriya: Thank you

Communication

Mujhe yeh samajh nahi aaya: This is beyond my comprehension.

Kripya madad karein: Please help me.

Mujhe yahan pahunchane ke liye kitna waqt lagega?: How long will it take to reach here?

Directions and Numbers

Ek (1), Do (2), Teen (3), Char (4), **Paanch (5):** One, Two, Three, Four, Five

Dahin / Bayen: Right / Left

Aage / Peeche: Ahead / Behind

Food and Dining

Ek chai / Ek coffee: One tea / One coffee

Yeh kya hai?: What is this?

Mujhe yeh acha laga: This was enjoyable.

Emergency and Help

Mujhe madad chahiye: I need help.

Police / Hospital kahan hai? : What location is the police/hospital station?

Bachao! Madad!: Help! (in case of emergency)

Miscellaneous

Kitna hai?: What is the price?

Kya yeh acchi jagah hai ghoomne ke liye?: Is this a good place to visit?

Kya aap English mein baat kar sakte hain?: Can you speak in English? You may find these words and phrases useful when visiting Varanasi. Even using basic words or phrases, conversing with locals in their language usually results in a friendly greeting and demonstrates respect for their way of life. To improve your overall travel experience in Varanasi and to facilitate communication, practice these simple phrases.

Fond Farewell to Varanasi and Recommendations

As you say goodbye to Varanasi, think about using these phrases to show your appreciation and gratitude:

Fond Farewell Phrases

Dhanyavaad Varanasi: Varanasi, thank you.

Main kabhi bhool nahi sakta: I have this lasting memory.

Aapka aashirwad sada saath rahe: May your blessings linger with me forever.

Alvida Varanasi: Farewell to Varanasi.

Recommendations and Suggestions

Share Your Experience: To encourage others to visit this vibrant city of culture, think about sharing your memories and experiences of Varanasi with friends or on social media.

Recommendations: Tell other travelers about the locations you adored, the unusual experiences you had, or the undiscovered treasures you found.

Express Gratitude: Give thanks to the locals, tour leaders, and other individuals who helped to make your visit unforgettable. Those who helped you have a great experience may greatly appreciate your gratitude.

Reflect on Your Journey

Reflection: Think back for a moment on your spiritual and cultural travels through Varanasi. Accept the experiences and knowledge you gained from your visit.

Gratitude for the Experience: the city for the deep spiritual and cultural immersion it offered.

Conclusion

Many travelers have a special place in their hearts for Varanasi because of its spiritual aura, diversity of cultures, and unforgettable experiences. As you say goodbye to this holy city, treasure the memories, impart your wisdom, and depart with a heart full of appreciation for the experiences Varanasi gave you.

Printed in Great Britain
by Amazon